To Juery,

FRAGMENTS
OF A WOMAN'S LIFE

Enjoy,

Sandra M.

Also by Sandra Manigault

The Book for Math Empowerment: Rethinking the Subject of Mathematics

FRAGMENTS
OF A WOMAN'S LIFE
A Memoir

Sandra Manigault

Godosan Publications, Inc.
Stafford, Virginia

Published by

Godosan Publications, Inc.
P.O. Box 3267
Stafford, Virginia 22555
(540) 720-0861
e-mail: sandra.manigault@gmail.com *om*

Library of Congress Catalog Card Number: 00-90049

ISBN: 0-9658541-1-6

Cover art by Sandra Manigault
Cover design by Terry Gallagher
Textual art by Donald Manigault

Printed in the United States of America

10 9 8 7 6 5 4 3 2 1

To Dawn and Patrick

Ma raison d'être

Acknowledgements

To

Donald, for showering me with love and understanding, and generously sharing his art throughout this book
Dawn and Patrick, for being a source of joy and continuing my legacy
Daddy, for being my friend as well as my father
Mama, for sharing her faith with me over three decades
Elle K. Iszard, for sharing her editorial insights so beautifully and bringing harmony to these essays
Terry Gallagher, for designing a fabulous book cover
Jeanene Noll, for copy editing the final draft with such patience
Laura Casal, for encouraging this project
B. J. Plenty, for excellent photography
My fellow writing students, for seeing beauty in these essays
My dear, dear friends, for giving my life color and texture.

Contents

*The beautiful art and graphics
are the creation of
Donald Manigault.*

Foreword

*H*ow wonderfully the Universe works! Ask for something and a better thing is granted! As always, I petitioned for financial freedom. However, needing a rest convinced me that I needed a sabbatical, a form of pay without work.

I had appreciated my 3-day workweek, but needed to get whole again. "See where you are." The words of Dr. Wu, my acupuncturist, stayed with me. It was he who taught me to write away grief and read away stress.

When I last took his advice, I spent a summer stowed away upstairs uncovering the joys of reading. I discovered the works of Mark Matabane, Gloria Naylor, Ben Okri, Alice Walker, Octavia Butler, and others. This time, on this sabbatical, I wrote my own stories --- the fragments of experience that made up my life.

Joy and Happiness

By Donald Manigault
circa 1969

Part One

The Players

Joy and Happiness

By Donald Manigault
circa 1969

Remembrances ----- *My parents*

Jacqueline

*W*hen she was a young woman, my friends would always remark, "Your mother is so pretty." Her beauty then was partly composed of her vitality and joy. Her picture still conceals the mystery behind her smile, a smile I never understood. It seems broader now. In fact, it is permanent upon her ageless face in the portrait. Edward saw the same smile the day he imagined her standing over his sickbed. I see a beauty in it now that I never fathomed when she was still with us, for she was never still.

Her hands were constantly moving. She had a peculiar way of wringing them. Her handwriting, likewise, was unusual and jagged. She had a funny way of vertically moving her pen back and forth, very fast, before she wrote anything. It was a gesture I could not understand. Her thoughts, like her writing, were busy, and leaped forth in sharp spurts.

"I suppose you told them all of your business," she threw out. Her words could jolt you like a fast slap on the back or in the face. Loving you meant that there were no parameters on what she could say. Her love freed her, and if you accepted it, you got both sides of it, the smooth and the spiky.

Discussing her (or what she had said) was tantamount to telling family secrets, a major betrayal for which you dearly paid. You could not lie about it for self-protection either, for you were convinced she would discern the truth. After a few verbal whacks to clear her conscience, you were safe, that is, until *you* triggered another salty response.

Her generosity was always luxurious, as I think back, not just toward my father and me, but toward everyone. There were frequent surprises and gifts of unsurpassed thoughtfulness, such as tickets to a coveted Broadway play when you came to town or serving dishes to match your expensive china. Even her grandchildren benefited enormously. However, what I never understood was what happened to the joy as I matured? Why did she begin to withdraw from me once I became an adult? While some things remained the same, others could not have been more different.

Dichotomies, the wonderful and the irritating, had embodied themselves in her psyche, each more entrenched than the other. She kept you emotionally alert for each new round of "love ball." She fully embodied the uniqueness the Universe has promised each of us. I never thought I would miss the spirit of the games the month her life ended.

She was always the queen of the cliché. Her wise words were often scoffed by the immature woman, but recently, I have come to marvel at their simple truth. Several I have forgotten, but some I remember clearly. As I age, the hidden aphorisms reintroduce themselves.

"A rolling stone gathers no moss," was one I ignored in my professional life. I can count the number of jobs I have had. Only the present one have I kept for any substantial length of time.

"Everyone who smiles at you is not your friend," was one I understood only in my 30's after being hurt many times by people who were friendly whom I misjudged to be trustworthy. I have outgrown that once desperate need for friendship. I love my friends, but can do very well without constant companionship. It has taken much time, but, with one exception over the years, I have become much less needy.

Her answer to people who over talked out of insecurity was, "An empty barrel makes a lot of noise."

Mom knew that their chatter was meaningless. I've met many empty barrels. Getting away from the "empty barrels" has always been difficult for me even when I knew after one or two sentences that they were about to waste my time. Now it causes me to ask, "Did I really respect the time of others? Or, to what extent have I bored my adult children by fretting over them in their presence?"

There are other "truths" I cannot recall now. They will probably resurface later as I go about the routine of living.

Silas

$\mathscr{A}$s he approaches the door with a smile, one can see the years he has lived. He has not been crushed by time, but the years have drawn him in. His face is both kind and sad at the same time. His eyes are reservoirs of emotion. There is so much he does not share, as if his role is to hear and see and record for an audience of one. His hair has thinned to where it exists only on the sides by the ears and on the back of the head. His chest, once robust, has sunken somewhat, and he seems much shorter than I remember. His clothes, although clean and matched, fit somewhat awkwardly, the belt gripping the pants by obligation. His hands are not soft, but enlarged and muscular. His talks to us patiently, methodically, as if each word needs to be weighed carefully, as not to offend. It is his way.

When I call him today, his voice is happy and enthusiastic. I believe that it is as much a matter of training as spirit. Helen is not there today, so he is glad for the company, and I offer it generously.

*𝒟*ear Daddy,

I have not been much of a letter writer. However, some things need to be said, given what a wonderful father you are.

In all of the years I have been on the planet, I have seen all kinds of fathers, and the surprising thing is only their children know what they are really like. (The rest of the world is left to speculate.) In general, men are very adept at presenting an empowered face to the outside world, while their foibles and insecurities remain blatantly obvious at home. Thank you for being a quiet, gentle giant of a man.

As a woman I've met all kinds of men: weak men, insecure men, boring men, entertaining men, sick men, stable men, nuisances, predators, etc.; men who think that because they earn a lot of money they are better men. That is hardly the complete measure of a man. Because of you, I know how to measure a man's greatness.

A great man is one who puts the well-being of his family above all else, someone who loves them, protects them, stands by them, and in front of them --- shielding them from a world that would thoughtlessly crush them. A man is someone who defines his success by the success of his family and its survival.

You don't have many letters behind your name, but I have some for you: Silas L. Young, M.A.N. extraordinaire. You have been a pillar of strength for all of us in an unassuming and quiet way. Thank you for the loving, patient care and the humility with which you always took care of Mom and me. Beyond being a wonderful father, you are a great man. Your positive energy and loving spirit have always been a stabilizing factor for the little family Donald and I have created.

I don't know if you recall, but many years ago when Patrick was visiting, he had no dress shoes with him for church. I asked Mommie if he could possibly wear a pair of yours. Mommie wisely answered, "I doubt if he could fill your father's shoes. Very few people could fill your father's shoes, Sandra." I sincerely hope he does one day, both in his own family and in his life path.

I love you always.

Sandra

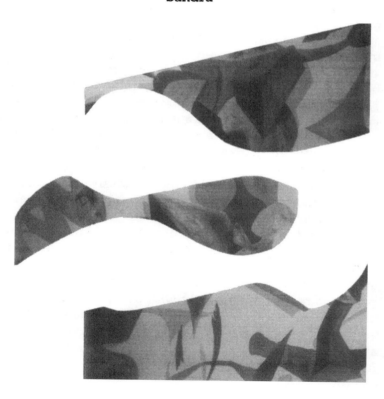

Mama

*W*hen you are young and newly grown you think that you know everything and that everyone ought to respect you. You are still naïve and fresh but think that you are sophisticated and, oh, so glamorous! And you think that looking the best you will ever look counts for a lot. Such was I when I first met the woman who would turn me, the child woman, into an adult woman. Such was Mama, Donald's mother.

Actually, I met Mama before I met Donald. It happened on the steps of my church. As a college student, I had just been recognized for something, and she congratulated me after the service as I descended the outside steps to leave. I remember our meeting because I remember being distracted by something. I remember accepting her congratulations politely, but coolly. She was with her son Ted, at the time, the man who would become the eldest of my four brothers-in-law.

When Mama and I met again, it was in the dining room of her home years later. After dating me for several weeks, Donald finally consented to bringing me home to meet his family for a Sunday dinner. She greeted me so warmly, as if she knew who I was to become in her life.

At first I did not really believe her when she said, "You will be a daughter." But, her capacity to love me while I grew up was boundless. I learned at her feet and from her eyes, and, because I respected her ability to see the inside, I learned quickly. She was powerful back then, twenty plus years ago, and her ability to "read" did not frighten me. In fact, I found it fascinating to watch her do it. It was far deeper than eye contact, for she would become very still and her gaze would deepen unblinkingly.

We spent long hours together "visiting" on the phone after Donald and I moved to Virginia.

We had a friendly relationship with only a short wall between us, which I carefully placed. This wall continued for three years into the marriage and came down with Patrick's arrival.

When Patrick was less than three months old we did something foolish. We moved. There was no one to help me adjust to the new baby, or to help Donald adjust to a new position. I remember Mama coming to visit us and giving us a silver cornucopia. It was a very gracious gift at the time and we did prosper. Even with three hundred miles between us, she and I became the best of friends.

Donald

*W*hen I first met Donald, I was attracted to his persona. He reminded me of a Mexican cowboy, because he always wore three-piece suits with a stringed tie, and boots. He still has those Mexican boots --- fine leather, custom made. He was charming, but did not have a "line," and he talked about things I never talked about before --- philosophy. He was not quoting the thoughts of other philosophers; he was discussing his own. I remember telling my mother what he said to me on one of our dates, and her response was, "He said *that*?" On another occasion, while attending a formal dinner somewhere, we sat at a table with six other people and listened to speeches, but I don't remember the people or the speeches. What I remember is *how Donald ate*. He cut the chicken off the bone like a surgeon doing very precise work. My children still laugh at that story ----"Mom fell in love, attracted to how Dad cut chicken!" I smile when I hear that version of it.

Donald always had a deep sense of purpose. Most of us ask, "Why are we here?" at some appointed time. Donald lives as if he asks the question every day. He taught me to read metaphysics and to think for myself, to be aggressive and to live without fear. He also taught me to say, "I love you," for no special reason except that it is true. And he loves his children with an uncommon valor.

Donald is also full of special surprises. Whenever I return from a trip, something new has been done to the house. One day, I returned to find the living room wall turning a bright shade of blue. On another, I awakened to find my abstract painting, which I thought had been ruined, completed into a masterpiece, that was later sold at an art show.

One day, not very long ago, I was looking for something to paint. All the canvases in the house had been used, and one alone was uncolored. I asked him, "May I paint on your canvas?" However, his thought forms upon the canvas were too unlike mine, too abstract. I changed them.

I must have begun to paint on the canvas of his life many years ago and he upon mine. One cannot marry and remain unchanged. It is the nature of the union. I have mellowed.

Dawn

*H*er soft hazel eyes cry out for understanding and love. She is not alone, but feels as if the world has isolated her. She reminds me of myself: the summer my feelings could no longer be contained in the body I had known all my life. It is hard to live normally with one's emotions screaming in a dozen directions.

"Be still," I tell her, "and say your prayers. Use the affirmation I gave you. It will calm your spirit." She says that she will, but somehow, I doubt it.

Her body has thinned. Still elegant, still beautiful, she makes a striking entrance in every room she enters. Heads turn. Eyes stare, as if to say, "From where did this magnificent creature come?"

She is abundantly talented --- writing as well as she draws. "One day," I tell her, "your work will be famous. It is very marketable, for your style has serious commercial value."

Her dancing has crossed the threshold of professional quality. She feels the music and the rhythms. Unlike some of her stage partners, whose work is technically correct but mechanical, Dawn's springs alive. The emotionality of her expression is mature and seasoned, as if she has lived a very long time. Her choreography moves superbly across the stage.

"I wonder," she questions, "if my piece is too advanced for the girls I've chosen to dance it?" I cannot answer her and conceal my disappointment that she will not be centered among them in the performance.

"I love you Mama." She kisses my cheek.

"I love you too, Sweetheart. Be happy. It will work beautifully," I respond.

We hug. I leave thinking, how beautifully formed is my daughter.

𝒟ear Darling,

Each year when you go back to college, I try to remember what there is that I have not told you the year before. College, my dear, is an appendage of the real world. It is blunt, cold, distant, and sometimes unfriendly. There are many faces and lots of laughter, but very little real friendship to be found, and when it is found, it comes from places that you do not anticipate. Be aware of the hype and lies. Everyone out there is lonely no matter with whom they are laughing and partying. Egos prevent them from disclosing that fact. Crowds change from year to year. I can remember years when I had no friends, and years when it seemed that I had several. Nevertheless, by now, all have vanished. And I do mean all. From my college none remains and from graduate school, only one, and I have not written him in about seven years.

Life moves us about in different directions. Remember Carleene, who was my best friend in high school, with whom I lost contact the year after you were born? As you know, I encountered her by accident at the airport in Denver and hardly recognized her. By the time we reconnected, all of the energy that once connected us had changed. Just like that --- poof! This is not to say that you should take life with a grain of salt. However, do not take every part of it so seriously. The present becomes the past very quickly.

Let's talk about the other side of humanity: men. They are human some of the time. I really believe their mothers raise them to be good and honest people, to have integrity and to be sincere in their dealings with others. However, when it comes to sex, their scruples bite the dust. Sincerity becomes deceit. Honesty becomes trickery and they tell lies, lots of them. They cannot help themselves. They are ruled by a different drummer; and, for this reason, do not trust them in matters of the heart to be truthful.

Your brother is different. We raised him differently. We did not raise the others you are now meeting.

Use your intuition and trust it. Do not go against it for anyone. Use your head and tell your heart to be quiet except to pump blood. In that way you will keep your sanity and peace of mind.

Do not be concerned if you are the only one who does not have a boyfriend. So what! Those who do are probably not very happy with them anyway. Of all the men I met in college and graduate school, only one made a great boyfriend. He was about 25 years old and had already grown up. That's one in six years. So take your time and be very choosy.

Remember who you are and continue trying to define your purpose for being here. That will give you focus and stamina and strength. You are special and I love you just the way you are. You have been blessed with many creative talents and that is not something to take for granted. Treasure them and develop them. They require time and energy for nurturing. Keep your own counsel and stay connected to the Source. Last of all remember, "We've got your back!"

Much love always,
Mom

To Patrick,

Son,

You will always be my champion.
Time has separated us in form only.
You will lead the life you are meant to live.
You have grown into a magnificent man:
Strong, tall, handsome, intelligent, kind, good.
I could not be more proud of who you are.

Remember the tree, and outstretch it.
Remember the sun, and outshine it.
Remember the moon, and exceed its peace.
Remember the wind, and match its strength.
We love you. I love you, now and always.

Mom

Part Two

Habitat

Setting

*W*here I live exists a spot of land and water where I go to relax. I enjoy watching the water and its flow as the breezes dance upon the surface. The boats docked here are quiet, for their owners are all off to work in places far different from this one. The ducks slowly sail by in pairs and occasionally some birds disrupt the silence. Fortunately, today I hear no human voices in this place.

The trees that surround the water on both sides converge into the distance. Some are the color of new green --- bright but tentative. Others bear the brown of winter. The mossy grasses of the flatlands are still pale and dry looking.

Few places here are as peaceful as this sleepy marina. I have come here often to write, sometimes anguished and confused. This, fortunately, is not one of those times. Today I dozed and awakened to hear the still silence of the mid-afternoon.

I have learned that peace and patience make a good tonic to undo the anxieties of life. As we move through our lives, the world has a habit of catching us by the heel and tripping us headlong into dissonant agendas. We get busy --- so busy that we lose our own rhythms. That is why I need the songs of nature to remind me of what my rhythms are. I am not whom I used to be back then when I lived on the outside of my soul and ignored its center. In those years I saw myself defined by what I did and where I was: how I dressed and where I thought I was headed. Those versions I have learned to put away. I have learned to halt the tide of life and look to its essence where I find simplicity and light --- beingness.

I have learned to write propelled by music of a familiar nature: chanting. The chanting once spoke to my sadness and is no longer necessary. But, I replay it on occasion. The sounds of the piano are comforting now that I no longer have to play it. It has become a favorite instrument, second only to the pan flute and harp.

Much has changed. Although life still throws its challenges, I like what it has become.

On Being a Woman

$\mathscr{I}$was never prepared for the onslaught of motherhood. That it would change my life was always an issue for me, for I always expected the change to be catastrophic. That was probably the why and wherefore of the strange tension that existed between Patrick and me. In desiring to keep his energies from controlling me, I built a wall between us, which took many years for me to peek over.

On the other side was a sweet and gentle-spirited lad with a ready smile and hesitant voice --- a voice which struggled to be understood and accepted. He did what I asked of him. He was good. His grades were superior. He sang in chorus and, in school politics, played the leader. He also bonded with his father and loved me from a safe distance.

I remember his first public performance. We were seated on the gym bleachers, undergoing the ritual of a school recital. Patrick had the solo in "The Christmas Song." He sounded absolutely wonderful to me. For he had hidden his (quite beautiful) singing voice. It would be many years before I would hear him do a solo again.

Patrick is grown up now. He is still handsome, still gentle spirited, but he has become strong also. He has developed a strength that is very admirable and formidable at the same time. He chose to study physics, the most difficult subject I can imagine, and struggles even now to earn a Ph.D. in that subject. I know he will succeed as he has done in everything.

We are friends now. We became friends actually when he was in high school. Loving a child, I have learned, does not mean that you have to control him. Only that you believe in him enough so that he will control himself.

Self observation

$\mathcal{T}$he pores of the skin on my hands stare back at me, hundreds of dry little webs crisscrossing at various angles. The nails too look abandoned: ragged, pale, and dry. They also lack attention.

As I look before the present, how could I have lived differently? The day held insufficient hours for me to care for family, home, job, self. Even now with all of these hours to myself, I get pushed aside to let some minor chore creep forth to plant itself in the center of my day. Perhaps I am addicted to routine matters which once done mean nothing except to indicate fulfillment of one's mundane obligations.

My body looks tired, but my face carries the years well, or so I am told.

My children are grown. I did not believe that would actually happen because the energy they created in the present (back then) was so terribly overwhelming. It was easy to lose sight of myself with them standing in the center of my life. They set the agenda. I do not regret it, but it does compel me to imagine how I shall make up the time I gave away to them.

I did not abandon everything. Donald and I had our share of dates and parties. These were fitted in alongside reams of homework, reports, and projects, as well as countless hours of time devoted to kid stuff. My own hours for play and reflection went unnoticed, almost. In a few quick moments of meditation I would find my center and lose it quickly the next day.

They have turned out very well.   Dawn dances. Patrick does research. They could have easily reversed their roles in another setting. I watch them go about seeking favor in their work and I feel proud of them and of our shaping their futures. They are without doubt our greatest achievement.

The Dance Class

*I*t is a cloudy, cold Friday, a damp and uncomfortable day. Normally this is a kind of day in which I do not feel like doing very much. However, this day is different and I am in a very different kind of place. The room in which I sit is large, very large. It must be 60 X 60 X 30 cubic feet or more, and the walls are very white with huge picture windows running along one boundary and full length mirrors adorning the opposite wall. The high ceiling is dotted with theatrical lights of all sorts as if performances were a common practice here. It is airy and clear and filled with energy unlike that in any class I have ever taken.

In this beautiful space filled with beautiful bodies I am experiencing clear insights. Throughout my life, I have had misgivings about the purpose of the body. Today, my vision is changed. The body is not, as I have for so long imagined, an instrument of the mind only. The body is a thing unto itself. The body is supposed to be breathed, to be moved, and to bend precisely as the mind instructs it; and it does this beautifully. The body should respond like a moving work of art. That is what I see here: grace, strength, discipline, joy.

In this massive lab are 25 – 30 dancers. Only one is male. They are not dressed as one would expect. In fact, all seem to be covered in old clothing --- light sweat pants and socks. A few are wearing leotards, but only the tops of those are visible. There is a piano in the room, but its keys are played only briefly. The instrument of choice is the drum. These experienced ballet dancers are warming up and dancing to the drum! It is an unusual combination.

They begin on the floor, almost yoga like, with their pixie-like teacher moving sprightly among their prone bodies, lightly adjusting heads and shoulders. As they stand, the energy in the room expands. They stretch and celebrate life. They run, leap, and celebrate their bodies. They can do so much, so perfectly, and with such magnificence. They are blessed, for this is how they manifest their lives, and my daughter is fortunate to be one of them.

In this square place where the ceiling has no limit, where the drumbeat mirrors and accelerates the heart, I see that life has more meaning as one "moves out of one's head." One lives to move. One moves to live.

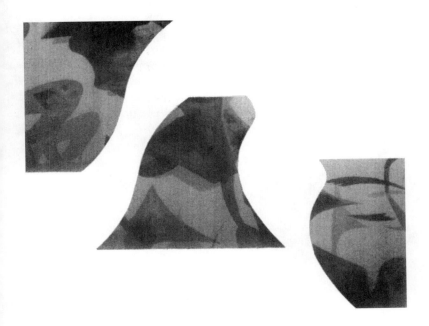

Part Three

Fragments of Memory

Snatches of Memory

$\mathscr{I}$must have been about seven when I saw really big houses for the first time.   In the little city of Washington, N.C., which Mommie and I visited periodically, we were in a car caravan traveling to the town's "black" beach. In crisscrossing town, we passed those big "white" houses on Market Street. They were only southern style colonials with big pillars and porches. But, in the eyes of a little girl from the projects, they were mansions, regal and untouchable.

As I drive past them now, they are still big, still regal, and seem as unreachable now as they were decades ago. The "white" part of town is sprinkled now with a few black families. The lawns remain impeccably manicured with huge pink and white azaleas overgrown and spreading lavishly on the grounds. The houses sit far back on the properties and are very quiet, as if no one is to be seen entering or leaving. Even Daddy's property, in the midst, sits on a freshly cut acre of verdant green bordered by huge old trees and flowering shrubs of various types. As I walk the neighborhood, there remains a quiet chill to be felt.

The inside of a church looks different when you are in the pulpit. Size becomes overwhelming, especially when scores of strange faces are reflecting your own thoughts. This church, although now empty, is no exception. It is not totally familiar to me, although it should be. It was founded by my great-grandmother, Grandma Sally, many years before I existed. For all of its years it remains a resplendent structure. The floors are richly covered in wine-red carpet that matches the covering on the pews. Crisscrossing scaffolding guts across the ceiling in stained mahogany and matches the wood trim around stained glass windows. The lectern in the pulpit is bounded by several rich green-leafed plants and three five-foot crosses decorated for Easter, mummy-wrapped in white linen. Five upright minister's chairs sit behind the lectern, no doubt to be filled tomorrow by various messengers of God. The sunlight, first beaming brightly upon our faces, now shines weakly as the afternoon closes.

The choir, now singing, is small. In fact, only five members are here to practice for Easter Sunday. All look worn by the years they have lived. Age plays a big factor; but the lack of ease experienced in their lives plays the larger role, I believe. The organ master is gray-haired and slender. He is the color of dark chocolate, and his fingers, although slender, are knotted. He is very accomplished and can transpose songs to a different key in the time it takes him to decide to do so. One woman wears a blue cotton scarf atop an auburn wig. It adds to the age she is working to conceal. Another wears a beret covering very short hair. They are all over sixty and sing gallantly for their sizes and number. Daddy, almost eighty, and seated next to me, sings best of all.

Continued

ℂn this historic church, the pipe organ is a thing unto itself. The sounds are deep and guttural. The pipes themselves are housed in a magnificent cage of oak behind the pulpit. This ornate structure must be eight by six by fifteen feet. The pipes, visible to the front, are an intricate bronze covered with blue, gold, and brown lattice work. The wood is beautifully carved topped by resplendent oak crowns. It is a soundboard that is aesthetically pleasing and resonant.

Looking at the little girls, now assembled for Easter, I had forgotten how pretty they can look on Easter Sunday dressed in lacy linen and satin dresses, flowery hats and more ribbons adorning freshly styled hair; socks with more lace and more ribbons. Did I cheat my own children, I wonder, by not submitting to this shopping ritual *every* April? If so, we were negligent in those early days before we moved to our current destination. Once the big house was completed, I believe all was rectified.

Clairvoyance

*B*efore it was ours, I saw our home in a dream ---
twice. In the first, Richard, Donald's student and mine,
had disappeared. There had been no clues as to his
whereabouts when, suddenly, I dreamt of his return. He
came to us in a "quiet harbor" to tell Donald that he finally
understood what Donald had been trying to teach him in
his meditation classes.

In the second dream were many fragments of my
life. Donald and I were standing together in a light
snowfall, kissing. We had just motivated a great audience
and were back home and very happy. In his hair was a
generous sprinkling of white --- snow or gray, I could not
tell. But, his skin, like mine, was very smooth. On my
back was a luxurious mink coat, and in front of us, a
colonial house, very large and majestic. The dining room,
which faced us, contained two long windows and seated
behind them were Patrick (at about age six), Mommie, and
a baby daughter. The baby squirmed restlessly in
Mommie's arms. However, Mommie sat there,
unperturbed by all of the child's energy, and very sad, as
if Daddy were no longer with us. Except for one, all of the
fragments of the dream came true.

The mink coat arrived first. It was delivered to our
house in Centreville in a large box for my mother. Even
the collar was the same. Dawn, the baby in Mommie's
arms, was born two years later, two years before we ever
sat in front of our long dining room windows. We have
been giving those motivational talks for many years now.

It always amazes me that when I walk down the
street from our house I still enjoy seeing the water. There
are no big boats. However, not far off, if you look in the
distance, from the hill, is a very quiet marina.

Memories

$\mathscr{I}$t is hard to be glamorous after you have been pregnant. The stomach is the greatest offender. It is no longer presentable. There is also the matter of time for one's own enhancement, which no longer exists as something one can take for granted. One's environment is captive to the imagination of a toddler, or six-year old, and the paraphernalia of child rearing. Toys abound, and strip one's pocket of loose change.

I remember the stiff little men who traveled with us in Patrick's hands whenever we left the house, and Dawn's Smurfette and pound puppies, like the one that got her into trouble that Christmas. I knew we were spoiling both children, but it did not last. They grew up.

I remember Patrick's disappointment, at age two, the day we sat outside in the misty air, in Annandale, experiencing a special presence --- an angel --- when suddenly, I snatched him indoors, afraid of cold and chill. There are mistakes.

I remember a time after dieting off thirty pounds. I had taken eight-year old Patrick swimming, in Manassas, and had worn a fuchsia bathing suit that showed curves I had not seen in years. A man tried to approach me through my son. Where do you live? What's your mother's name? It was quite amusing actually.

I remember. I remember the surprise on Patrick's face when he got his first leather jacket for his fourteenth birthday. Surprises are sometimes wrapped in benign deceit. I can still feel the glee I felt at seeing something beautiful and sending him scurrying through the mall with Dawn on a concocted errand. I had his gift wrapped first in men's paper and then again in baby paper and said it was a present for someone's shower.

That hidden birthday surprise was such a great and wonderful gift that Dawn got a present also as not to be outdone. In the moment of discovery, Patrick's smile was the brightest I had ever remembered.

The Miracle of Life

*S*ometimes you don't know that you are pregnant, only that your body is different. Changing. There is swelling everywhere. The body becomes outrageously distended and awkward. You are uncomfortable, but still trying to look "cute."

It is not the same for everyone. I remember Minja, at Donald's surprise birthday party, nine months pregnant, looking absolutely alluring. Later I heard that she was the talk of the table, among the men, at dinner.

I remember myself, at nine months pregnant, photographed by the pond in Chantilly, happily wearing a denim dress over an elephant.

Busy. Too busy to notice that your body has prepared for birth, you suddenly go into labor. The rules don't apply and the birth training seems obsolete in these moments. Your angels are born and are wonderfully precious. They struggle to grow up. You struggle with being grown. Life changes: no longer yours, but theirs.

Patrick and Dawn are a charming pair, staring back at me from their portrait in the living room. Priceless jewels. How much is them? How much is us?

I see them now in my mind's eye. At twenty-seven and twenty-one, respectively, they are indeed miracles, magnificent and resplendent in every way.

New Memories and Old

$\mathscr{I}$t is a sleepy entry into Thursday. My mind remains focused on the images of last night's dreamscape. Mommie and Sister were in it in our old house on 142nd Place, in Queens. It is a family party, almost a reunion, and the camaraderie I sense, is very warm and special. I belong, as do they. I hugged a tall man the way one hugs a man who is not a relative. I remember seeing him as very thin. But, who was he?

I choose not to think often about growing up on 142nd Place. The memories I have of Mommie's friends there are happy ones. The memories of my own are not. Ten, eleven, twelve are awkward ages in the life of a young woman. They are the ugly duckling years when one is waddling into womanhood and feeling awkward around boys and shunned by girls. I remember taking on several insecurities at this age.

It was both stimulating and intimidating to be surrounded geographically by so many boys at the time. I can still see the all black cast --- pretty girls, leggy boys, always walking from Foch Boulevard to Rockaway on a mission to nowhere. High drama.

Fragments of Memory

*M*ommie always had a lot of class. That is what I saw. That is what others saw. She was a woman who knew what to do and what made sense; what was appropriate and what reflected good taste. She had an overabundance of common sense. She never sneaked around to do anything. If she was going to do something, she was impeccably honest about it. She hated lying. Apparently, so did my father. Daddy always said, "If you'll lie, you'll steal."

They made a handsome pair. Daddy, as I remember, always had a small closet as I was growing up. He said he didn't need a lot of clothes as a policeman. Mommie, on the other hand, had a great many, shoes especially, shoes which never seemed to wear out; and thus, her collection grew. After both of them retired, his wardrobe seemed to catch up with hers.

They were always together. Mommie did not like to drive, even though Daddy had taught her well. Daddy, as I remember, was always practical. It appeared that he held the family purse tightly; but in fact he did not. I should have known that Mommie's generosity could not have existed without his input.

I remember Christmas as the most generous time of all while growing up. I can recall coming into the living room as a child and finding so many gifts that I did not know where to begin. It would take two hours just to get to all of them.

One Christmas, Daddy gave Patrick his first train set. It was the most beautiful and generous gift he could have been given. Patrick loved it and enjoyed it for many years. I remember many gifts from my parents over the years --- gifts of clothing, money, toys, time, and abundant love. Their generosity continued well into my children's adult lives.

Daddy is still extra generous to all of us. When Dawn told him she would be spending three weeks in Florida with the Urban Bush Woman summer dance program, Daddy readily mailed her $300. He is kinder than ever.

I will never be able to repay his kindness. But, perhaps there is something special that I can do for his 80th birthday. I bet he would really enjoy a surprise birthday party. A formal dinner for everyone who means something to him, in a very special restaurant, would be a perfect way to say "We love you."

"Not too much of a surprise," Helen said. "I'll tell him about it at the last minute. But, if I tell him earlier than that, he will tell us not to do it." Agreed.

Patrick flew up from Atlanta. The Pastor and his wife came. Dawn's new friend came, as did his parents. I finally got to meet Mr. Hoover, Daddy's best golf buddy. Evelyn brought Larry, who rarely ventures out since losing his leg. Scotty came and, as usual, looked like the family's most prosperous member.

God has a way of making things perfect. The restaurant was outstanding. The gifts were wonderful. The carrot cake and cheesecake were excellent. Tributes to Daddy were magnificent.

Part Four

Work

An Agreement With Myself

To become successful I must choose to face issues I have avoided. I must choose to let go those things that have held me hostage. To grow, to expand, I must release those beliefs that have corrupted my consciousness. I must relinquish negative habits of over-stimulation, over-feeding, numbing myself (with deafening music or mindless television), and other habits that destroy my sensitivity. I must reroute energies and reprogram thinking. I must stop letting others dictate how I should live and who I should be. I must free myself to be myself. I must get out of my own way. And I must get out of the way of others. I must let go of fruitless and unsatisfying relationships. I must learn to accept what I cannot change. I must stop camouflaging what I really want with empty activities. I must take responsibility for my life. I must choose to grow up. To be a success, I must adopt those lifestyle rituals that make others successful --- being decisive, focused, organized, realistic, determined, hard-working, patient, and serene.

The above essay was excerpted from
__The Book for Math Empowerment__

Editor

$\mathscr{T}$his spring I made peace with the job from hell. The job had come about suddenly back in 1985, a year I had been carelessly submitting resumes, looking for something to do, as if staying at home with Dawn, in this big house, were not enough.

Personnel called about 11:30 one morning, and I remember standing at the telephone in my bathrobe thinking, "They're serious."

The job was frustrating and over-regimented. We had four bosses, and although one of them was not really a boss, everything I wrote had to meet his specifications. Of him, I had Dracula dreams. He was one of those peculiar nuisances who made everything complex and who spoke in opaque riddles.

Although our team had not been hired to bewilder the public that is how we made our money --- revising the GED and creating new agendas for everyone. Only two of the original team remain today.

Recently, I offered to do a free-lance writing project for them, but not without the strain of anxiety, wondering if it would be good enough.

Fall Sunday

$\mathscr{D}$onald and I seem to be working all of the time. It took me awhile to recognize we were doing this, it had become so ingrained in our lifestyles. Today is a Sunday, one of those beautiful fall days when the sky is a clear blue and clouds appear only as the sun is setting. The insects are still in view, as are children playing basketball and soccer. Some husbands are spending the day tending to their lawns or shrubs. We have just seen off our best friends, the Blackshears, after an evening date and overnight visit. They, too, are hurrying home to work.

I ask myself, "Is this the plight of today's professional middle class? Always working? The more structured our day off, the better we like it?" I tell myself that with structure and schedules the hours fold together more lucratively, the payoff more apparent. But, is it really? My laundry is done, the floors vacuumed, my lessons planned, my tests written, my pages finished. I could do more: type 100 envelopes, finish a speech. But, the time has come to stop. My back cramps as I continue to work. My body exhibits more sense than my brain. Donald has three more hours of work ahead of him.

Classroom

*O*n a typical day staring back at me is a sea of intelligent faces. Perhaps my methods of motivating need changing.   Without abdication, there needs to be a realization that I don't teach.

It has been a good day.   We caught up in pre-calculus.   Yet, those who won't read do not catch up because they refuse to understand the process of learning. Too many people think that "to read" means "to skim." They ought to read math the way they read a love scene --- over and over again for the details!

Math 120 is working on systems of linear equations. I read their faces as I talk and see that some just cannot connect the ideas they hear.   It is as if their learning is fragmented, disjointed.   They are bored and probably are losing me every two sentences.

Anger? Anger!

*M*y students amuse me when they take a test. Some of them regress back to high school.

"Is this equation right, Mrs. Manigault?"

I answer honestly. "No!"

"Well, should it be ...?"

"I cannot give you any more information, only that it is not right."

Next, there is the unfamiliar face sitting in the back of the room. I could swear this face has not been here more than once. Students, such as these, fail by default. They quit coming, but never withdraw. In spite of all my admonitions on day *one* and in the syllabus, they refuse to follow directions.

There are additionally my more "mature" students, frozen with fear and clinging to the belief that math is hard and they will fail.

There are the "fragile females," women of privilege: privilege in the sense that they have made it to forty surrounded by excuses and abdicating responsibility for their own behavior. (Thank God I had none of these this semester! Yet, when I do, I ask myself, where do they come from? They surely did not grow up with the likes of my mother!) Such women are intimidated by age, subject, and by me. Not a good mix! In the effort to be both professional and structured, I succeed at scaring these timid types. Sometimes they report me to my supervisors for being "intimidating." Whatever do they expect: A smiling caricature that entertains?

I am uncharacteristically cold today. Perhaps I am upset. Am I allowed to react to the stresses of things not going right? The right, occasionally, to be human? Or, is the humanity of imperfection extended only to some of God's people?

Honestly, I do believe the world needs to learn a thing or two about people of color, especially successful, ambitious people of color: the ones who do not fit stereotypes, who are very secure and confident. When I attend workshops and luncheons for professional women's groups, especially professional African American women's groups, I see exactly what my students see --- an awesome array of well-spoken, well-dressed, affluent individuals.

These are not the images the media chooses to show America.

A Bad Day

$\mathcal{F}$all 1997 --- probably my worst semester. Too pushed, too busy, no space, no time. No time. Even fifteen minutes is a blessing. I do not like working like this. I have become very negative, very discouraged. I must turn it around, to begin to expect the best once again. It is important to clear the air. Maybe I have become too cynical. "I" keeps intruding. Have I become obsessed with self: my writing, my agenda, my time, my cellulite, my pain? Have I shut out the rest of the world? Why is there so little gratitude? What has happened to me? What has made me so tired?

How can I feel like myself again?

Part Five

*The Sabbatical Life and
Lessons Learned*

Parts

*I*ntuition speaks to us gently and quietly. I used to think it screamed with loud energy. I was wrong. It is a still, quiet voice, just as we were told. It probably gets loud only if we are in imminent physical danger. Sometimes as I am going about the day collecting supplies for an errand, I stop, focusing my attention on a single item. Subconsciously, I sense a quality of importance. "Never mind," I think aloud, dismissing the subtle nudge of my intuition. Later, arriving at my destination, I realize that this object is required after all.

My body talks to me also. It tells me when it wants to exercise and stretch. Sometimes it awakens me with a gnawing restlessness that forces me to get up before my brain is ready.

My mind listens. It enjoys searching the mesmerizing quiet of soundlessness: no music, no appliances, no traffic. I have not yet discovered what it is listening for.

Meditation

It has become a ritual for me --- writing. Today, the sun is at my back; I am late for this appointment. My inner self, my Higher Self, beckons daily that I meet with her first before the avalanche of trivial pursuits takes over and these chores masquerade as major events of the day.

This appointment occurs in a special place, the living room. I find this quite amazing, given that we never did much living here. The vibrations are uncluttered and warm. Peach carpet warms my feet and colorful furniture greets my eye. Love seats face, curtsy, and compliment each other trading pillows in coral and ivory, as if waiting for me to sit at the piano diagonally opposite my circular oak desk. Several photographs of our children survey the scene. Across the nearly empty foyer stands the dining room, marshalling the area with its elegantly appointed chandelier. Art is everywhere --- by contrast, very modern, very colorful, very majestic. Here each day I meet and contemplate the measure of my life. Today, I write without music, hearing only the rhythms of the house and the sounds of my own breathing.

Morning Writings

The voice with which I write is not all mine. It surpasses my speaking voice in time and dimension, almost as the superconscious mind goes beyond the conscious mind. It is mine to use and gives of its potential generously. The ritual of morning writing has come to fill a unique place in my life. Today, I veer from the course by writing before I clear the space in my waking mind. I should pause to "warm up" the imagination first.

I stop my writing to lend my time briefly to the radio bandits. I listen to a barrage of commercials in anticipation of the morning's first cash giveaway. The lucky name is not mine.

What is the difference between "morning pages" * and real writing? I have asked this of myself more than once. The "morning pages" are unedited babbling, a cleansing of the residual sludge that clogs the creative spirit. For me, real writing is more from the mind and less from the solar plexus, sometimes clearer, smoother, and less personal: pre-edited, but not more perceptive. For me, the "pages" make writers' block a past issue; this catharsis creates a flow at once controlled and yet almost spontaneous.

* "Morning pages" is a writing ritual, encouraged by Julia Cameron, in her book, The Artist's Way.

May Monday

𝒜t is one of those peculiar afternoons when the sun has reluctantly chosen to remain visible and the air inside is cooler than the warmer air outdoors. The baby leaves have grown to midsize, enough to fill out the barrier of trees behind our house. A black bird stands atop a dead limb, facing upright. His mouth is full of something orange and brown. A lone dog barks sullenly.

Today we were a couple. We walked and weeded the lawn together. I wrote some bills and then we drove out for honey coated peanuts. Every Monday should unfold as nicely as this one.

I read now while Donald tutors his second student. I have promised myself to paint today, possible only if I avoid engaging the television. My attention returns to what I am reading, a memoir costumed as a novel. The author conveys her story in the first person: memories recorded thoughtfully and with great delicacy. Her characters are dressed in blue and yellow cotton, as am I.

The afternoon sun has slipped away again. My solitary bird companion has been joined by five others who chirp quietly. Life goes on about its business.

A Lazy Afternoon

*W*e are finally at the park --- Leesylvania, an ugly name, a lovely park. Donald is pretending to be grumpy, rather to have stayed at home doing the ordinary. Not me. I could do a new adventure each day and stay at home only when it threatens to rain. I finished reading my novel yesterday. It contained just enough lust and scandal to read well.

As I sit here amidst the tall grasses of spring, the clouds hover over the water without any movement. They are full and billowy. Jet skiers break the soundless barrier in front of me. Although the enchantment of the river is challenged by the sound of an engine to my rear, the sound is constant and not very loud.

A young mother explores the river's edge with her daughters. Pretty in pink and white sundresses, they are well behaved and curious, happy to be here. With a stick, one of them spanks the water. They appear to be about four or five years old.

A few bees hover between the grasses and shoreline trees. They are big enough for me to see clearly in the distance.

The river makes small waves against the shore. Their crash is soothing to the spirit. Donald speaks to me, but I choose not to hear him. A stringed bug inches its way across my page. "Look at this!" I shout excitedly. My breath does not budge him.

Across the waters the sky is reflected blue. Miles away, but clearly visible, is another state. Decaying driftwood, like skeletal bones, line the shore. I pray, and the sun comforts me with a final caress. I am healed.

Returning

What will it be like to teach again?   Standing, emoting, cajoling students to do for themselves what only they can do.

The campus has had a gray and quiet aura each time I have returned. The offices looked tightly crowded after these spaciously appointed months at home where paper piles are few and easily discarded.

Finally, I have come to notice life's sweet treasures --- the racket of birds outside a window; a warm pillow snuggled against cold feet, a good neck rub. The world is a noisy place this quiet afternoon. At least I have the time to listen to it.

Post-sabbatical Musings

*D*uring this sabbatical, many days were spent at the library, an unlikely surrogate office. Many days began at my desk. Circular and perfect for journaling, it is artistically crafted and fits perfectly with the other treasures in our living room. On my desk sits a brass eagle, Dawn's ceramic rose, and a short stack of precious books. A greeting card stands conveying joyous thoughts. The light shining on my hand is bright and warm as I write. I am happy.

***

I love my work. I think that I have the best job that I will ever have. In life, I suppose you have to know when to quit looking for something better.

Summer school, this year, at NOVA, is good. My algebra class is large and mature, and the mix of students is interesting. They are an ethnic salad. Theirs is going to be a rich world; luxurious in shared experiences and social interaction. Dawn has already experienced a taste of that world in her circle of friends and associates at college. My world, at her age, was only black and white. Hers, like my students', is additionally African, Asian, Hispanic, and Middle Eastern.

I like these students. Apparently their test was not too difficult as they began leaving early on. Choosing not to teach after the test was wise. It gave them an extra gift --- time. Sometimes I worry that my tests are too rigorous, like my teaching. One half hour remains with only five students present. With this class, I can feel their respect and admiration.

Finding the Courage to Live

*W*hat many of us consider living, isn't. We go though rituals and follow habit patterns. Few unique things occur on a given day. Everything does not occur as planned, but is planned as it ought to occur. We are so afraid of not knowing what to expect that we are reluctant to venture beyond known parameters. We succeed at hemming in ourselves. We build good prisons.

There are also those of us who are afraid of rattling the sensitivities of family members or significant others. Good jailers they can make, especially siblings, in-laws and parents whose opinions we over cherish. We are like well-trained mice accustomed to scurrying through maze after maze in search of external approval. We remain dissatisfied while all others feel safe about our decisions.

We have a choice. We can continue to belittle our existence and aim to please, or we can stand up for our right to be ourselves, even if that entity is vaguely defined. We have much to lose but more to gain. In that valley of unknown experiences lies freedom --- freedom to choose without being captive to the presumed needs and desires of others. That is a false paradigm of our generation --- that the needs and desires of others should supercede our own, and that there is something mortally sinful about what is called selfishness. Not so.

If we are false to ourselves we suffer for it both now and in the hereafter. We must let go of people and habits that drain our life energies. We must say NO to what is outside our focus, our purpose. We are not dummies society winds up to trudge a mindless path called obligation. Freedom means defining who I am, what I do. It is and has always been my birthright.

61

Alternatives

 *T*elevision steals the life from many of us as it saps creative juices and deadens the spirit.   It would be entertaining, but too much of it is banal trivia.   Next is the issue of ongoing commercial interruption, more irritating on television than it is on the radio or the internet.   These intrusions break the flow of thought forcing us to live a staccato existence.

Perhaps that is the joy of *live* theater.   One is left alone to concentrate until there is an appropriate break --- intermission.

I marvel at how continuing live dance theater is. Perhaps it is even too connected.   A drama is catapulting across the stage in tune with music that keeps the emotional eye riveted to a handful of moving figures stretching, reaching, doing artful, amazing things with their bodies.   The audience wants to shout at the joy of it when the lights go black.   A call to applaud!   Before one recovers from one beautiful performance, another is rippling through the senses.   So fast!   So fast!   One's heart can barely keep up with the energy pumping across the stage!

The beauty of such unabashed creativity wakes the mind, willing it to bring the body alive --- up and out of the orchestra and onto one's feet!

Concert, May 1998

𝒟ear Dawn,

You have created dance to be complex, riveting, powerful, and beautiful. Last night's *"Truthful Facades"* was the best of show not because you are our daughter, but because you are an artist. You make beauty of life. Your poetry or visual art may move vividly on paper. However, when your poetry reaches us, in the audience, in choreography so magnificent, we want to shout "bravo," "encore," and see more of it unfold beautifully on the stage.

You create innovatively with none of the pale repetitions we see in other works. We were completely taken with your intensity and freshness, and the powerful synergy of music and movement. You have been blessed with a great gift.

In the audience I am always challenged. Whom do I watch? Can I take it all in? In your work, I loved the taking on of the façade, the soul's giving, the emotions erupting and cascading across the stage with such intensity. In the bodies of your dancers was **your** *spirit.*

Congratulations! We loved it and we love you!

Love always,

Mom

The Measure of My Life

$\mathscr{I}$have always wanted to be many things that I am not: gracefully slender, sensuously supple, a dancer, a master at combining color and flow and texture, an artist.

Although it is too late for me to become a dancer, I rejoice in Dawn's talent on stage. Few things bring me the joy I experience in watching her perform. When she was little, the feeling was one of amusement and pride. Now it is a feeling of rapture. She looks so wonderful and is everything a dancer would want to be.

My few paintings hang upon our walls. I remember having to fight to get them decently framed when our budget was low. While my fuchsia and purple abstracts hang beside the piano and in the dining room, not matching the creative impact of Donald's work, they belong. Some of my paintings scream for expression, having burst from my imagination in streaks of blue and orange, softened by mauve and purple.

Why is it so hard in life to do all the creative stuff the soul wants to do?

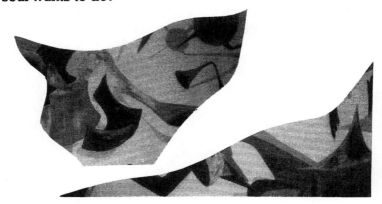

Thinking

*I*believe that hate is a real thing; that it lives in the belly of the solar plexus, right beneath the rib cage on the inside of the body. Not encased in the stomach, but transcending that physical organ, it minimizes itself into a small pit and waits. Later, it seethes through the pores without warning and poisons the future.

Fortunately for me, I never knew how to really hate. I knew, instead, how to hurt. Always inflicting myself with the wrongdoings committed by others, I learned early how to forgive them and blame myself instead for their infractions. I am certain many social encounters went unheeded in terms of the lessons they contained; missed opportunities to learn, instead turning themselves into sacred places of hurt.

My life has been good in spite of my psychological blind spots and reluctance to think fast with words.

Someone once told me it is as if I have sensors all over me: too perceptive of feelings and attitudes. Always knowing when something is wrong. Always inadvertently "getting into other people's stuff."

When I was a teenager, I would go to parties and be instantly uncomfortable much of the time. At the time, I assumed that I was too self-conscious. That was only partly correct. I was too *conscious*. However, having no one of the psychic variety with whom to communicate, I stayed in the dark about my own nature. What was strength I perceived as a weakness.

Dawn is likewise very intuitive, but more fortunate than I was at her age. She knows. And like the other women in our family, she is a wonderful friend and listener, and is extremely generous.

I wonder if all of us tend to give too much.

Space and Habitat

I have learned, finally, how to create my own atmosphere, to find at home what I used to venture outside for: stimulation. It consists of setting a mood driven by color, sound, and scent. Of writing by candlelight, feeling the joy of one's own space, relishing the uniqueness of the moment, being with oneself. This path leads into the reality of the soul, into one's own sense of spirituality, one's connection to life. This unison is difficult to establish because of all the man-made sounds in our environment. It is as if the machines kill the sense of connectedness. And the madness with which we clothe ourselves, the frenzy, kills it.

Solitude returns it. Beyond body, beyond mind is something beautiful, something new and ancient. The music of this age --- new age --- brings us back to peace. Listen.

Two eagles reside upon my desk, the brass one purchased not for myself, but for Donald. The other lives on paper and soars high in the clouds above a riverbed, beyond forested coastlines, towards its mountainous habitat. Inside the card are the words of my dearest friends from Vail: Vincent, Hind, Jerina, Sarah, Karen, Cecilia, Mukti, and Tom. Each greeting is its own special treasure.

Am I an eagle? Does my path soar way above the terrain upon which my parents set me? Going beyond the rudiments of teaching and into the psychology of learning would seem to leave an old boundary far behind. I have chosen to challenge the barriers people and society have erected.

The following is excerpted from
The Book for Math Empowerment

I am a child of God.

I am filled to overflowing with God's healing power.

I am completely healed in

mind, body, soul, spirit, thoughts, attitudes and emotions.

I am completely healed in the solar plexus center.

I am completely healed in the heart center.

I am whole. I am healed. I am free.

Thank God. Thank God. Thank God.

My book, ***The Book for Math Empowerment,*** sets the groundwork for a new era in education. It is the first of what will become a landslide. The competitors have not yet determined how to catch up.

I use music to create my virtual reality. Although I choose words to define a realm in which people can learn, I recognize that the abstract cannot be broached with the abstract. If opposites attract, the world of mathematics should be accessed through the disciplines of art and music. Affirmations should be planted subliminally behind music, or recited consciously with music, or both. Formulas should be concealed subliminally behind art, whole charts of math formulas, stoking the memory, day to day.

As I reread my own book, I see in chapter eight a realm of harmony and freedom humanity could embrace. Even for me it is a utopian state. I inch toward my own philosophy, aware that it is a spiritual ideal, that it foreshadows a perfected life.

I see success as freedom from what now is; freedom from a world scarred by dissonance. I see success as living in a world sparkling with joy, swept into a place of peace created out of our need for sanity. I see a world defined by serenity, by music. Spun upon the sweet plumes of harps and the softness of flutes, the birdsong of morning, the freshness of dew, the sound of sunlight sparkling on lake water.

On Rt. 95
10 PM

Trumpets sing sweetly.
Jazz reflects the rhythm of cars
Speeding though darkness.
Harmony ---
A marriage of driver and speed.
Music ---
Rhythmically strange, lyrically new.
Songs
With vanilla jazz and disco beat
Eating through pores like joy.

Hips rock, heads talk.

I love my car in the dark.

Part Six

Finale

Habitat II

This room has been my home for almost nineteen years. In spite of choices to be somewhere else: the kitchen, the living room, the back room, the office --- this is the place to which I return to relax. This is not where I write, nor where I sleep, but where I become one with myself.

The insects provide a soothing backdrop. I hear them by the thousands. They manage to stay hidden in the leaves, grounds, and trees of our backyard. It is like a jungle back there: a plethora of overgrown shrubs and weeds folded among dozens of trees of various types, falling over or leaning upon one another. Through the open sliding glass door, I watch the leaves dance gently in the morning breezes. Beyond the din of singing insects, a bird has its solo. Unlike the birds, the bug chorus has a constant chant.

It is like a call to weary minds to sit and abdicate the stress of living fast. Inside this room are furnishings with which I am overly familiar, each vying to provide greater comfort than the next. The wood framed chairs are of a pretty texture and color I have come to take for granted. The walls support our art, much too different in tone and color to live out their purposes side by side. The carpet is a smooth gray, which blends and matches the pin-striped love seat, which faces its counterpart in busy white. So much else is assembled for purposes of use, not my choice for beauty. However, in the arms of one well-placed chair, there is a knowing that, at this moment, everything that I need is already a part of whom I am.

Afternoon Musings/ P.M. writings

$\mathscr{A}$lthough it is not easy to admit it, I have become addicted to writing. It is as if I cannot begin the day or go far along in the day without doing it. I tell myself that I am only being a good pupil of Julia's and doing my assignments properly, but it goes beyond that now. It does not matter whether I am doing morning pages or just writing about what is around me; I have to do it. The way one feels when one is forced to leave the house without one's morning shower is how I feel if I do not write before I proceed with what I have to do. A quick spin around the page is not enough either. I have to be here for at least 25 minutes for the exercise to be meaningful.

In the "new" office, I face both windows and allow the spring breezes to blow in. The sun is dazzling here in the early morning hours, something I had not noticed.

Our home is not as bright as it was eighteen years ago. The baby shrubs Donald planted have grown to over twenty feet and hide much of the natural light. I tell myself I am impressed with how we live. Not luxuriously, but comfortably. Things are still neat and pretty. Dawn says that our family room needs help --- that it needs to be redecorated. That without all of this art the house could not stand as it is now. Perhaps she is right. Somehow, however, I am not concerned about that. I generally never was. Only once do I ever recall being driven about "fixing up" more than we did initially. Perhaps that is one of the by-products of being "house-poor," something I could not have admitted several years ago. I have always been more focused on what we were accomplishing, how the children were doing, how our classes were proceeding, etc. Not how the house looked other than being clean and uncluttered, with a reasonable amount of decorative touches.

Union

$\mathscr{T}$he birds are very noisy in the darkness. I have been listening to the cars leaving the Harbour for over an hour. Donald breathes loudly, making sleep impossible for anyone else. He is sleeping, but turns away from my invading hands. It is my way of stopping the noises he makes, but he has learned to resist.

I have come to love the sound the morning birds make. They have no respect for people who want to sleep. Between the breathing next to me, the birds beyond me, and the tension within me --- why do I lay here?

I don't like to sleep alone. Even when Donald is noisy beside me, I want the comfort of his body. It is a good thing to which I have grown accustomed: an essential part of this union.

Getting up when one is still tired, and not being able to lie in bed listening to the birds or to the rain, is one of the tragedies of modern life. Donald's breathing has quieted. He must be awakening. Now I can return to sleep.

Satisfaction

$\mathscr{I}$t has taken me many years, but I have finally come to determine what is good in life.

1.   Eating a great bowl of hot soup for a cheap price, slowly in a comfortable place.

2.   Savoring carrot cake, sweet and creamy, just the way I like it.

3.   Having Donald find the itchy spot on my back and being cuddly afterwards.

4.   Giving myself a book signing with important people in my life present.

5.   Laughing so intensely that it makes my stomach hurt.

6.   Seeing my daughter sparkle on stage at each stage of her life.

7.   Enjoying a crackling fire in a huge fireplace in the presence of good friends.

8.   Playing.

9.   Seeing my father remarry at the age of seventy-six.

10. Getting a professional massage from a man I have just met.

11. Watching the sun set behind gray and coral clouds.

12. Seeing Dawn and Patrick graduate from high school, college, and graduate school.

13. Getting a zero electric bill in the mail.

14. Teaching an SAT Prep Course we do not have to recruit.

15. Paying off our mortgage.

16. Enjoying Thanksgiving dinner that I do not have to cook.

17. Watching Dawn and Patrick together.

18. Taking the four of us to the Bahamas for Christmas.

19. Reading a whole novel in two days.

20. Sipping hot peppermint tea on a winter evening.

21. Finishing my first book and publishing it ourselves.

22. Seeing Donald dressed up and looking like a million dollars.

23. Wearing a dress that, for ten years, has not fit.

24. Understanding the phrase "peace of mind."

Foray Into Creativity
**This piece was written to accompany our first art show in the
September of 1995. It was a success.**

A creative rarely knows his own power. Donald Manigault, like so many of us, channeled life energies into academic and business pursuits. When the inspiration to do an art show emerged this spring, serendipitously, it brought to his work a new, dynamic energy. Esoteric from its very inception, Donald's style has grown, expanded, and matured over the latest works. More vibrant, more flowing, and much more colorful, his work exudes a powerful new energy. "Life-form," spiritual and mysterious, gives us a glimpse into the essence of matter. It writhes and metamorphoses so quickly that its ultimate end eludes us. The original "Star-child" was conceived with the birth of our son, Patrick. The new "Star-child," surrounded by its spirit guides, patiently awaits its entry back upon the planet earth where lessons in matter are learned.

An artist may frequently conceal what he really thinks, but, not in his art. That we see crosses protecting our planet, throughout this exhibit, tells us of Donald's unerring faith in the protecting Christ spirit, forever shielding and watching over our planet and all of its life forms. We need only acknowledge and thank that Power to maximize our own soul potential. We do not "see" the Universe guiding our every step. But, Love is always present. Revealed in the beautiful work "In His Hands" are not one but seven crosses protecting our planet. This work is the brainstorm of our daughter, Dawn, an artist in her own right, whose opinion we have come to value and cherish. (Thank you, Dawn, for a brilliant idea.)

Dawn has also been instrumental in helping her Mom get her own art launched. Not for sale in this exhibit is a striking vortex of fuchsia, purple, and gold, (seen in the living room), a birthing planet reminiscent of female creative energies. This first major work by Sandra was done this summer after a simple thrust from Dawn: "Go for it, Mom." Going to the High School of Music and Art was a long, long lesson in "wannabe" for Sandra. Now, the former "wannabe" artist has finally taken a first step. "Blowout," "Weaver," "Star-burst" and others in the exhibit represent other firsts. Sandra's works are dominated by a brilliant mixture of gold, fuchsias, and vast expenditures of energy and imagination. All are one of a kind. "Father and Child," she has to thank her husband for. Without his collaborative assistance this unusual convergence of blue realities would not exist. In this work, represented more subtly, are the mother and other essential life energies pivotal to the two central figures.

"Reflections," that magnificent ascent into color and shape, is one of Donald's finest works. Other works of interest are "Synergy," "Focus," and "Still Life" each a unique variation from Donald's former style. Fun runs rampant in the singular works "Trilogy" and "Evolving Rhythms," another collaboration. ***Enjoy!***

Driven to Write

" *E*veryone's got a book in them." However, getting it written is difficult and getting it published is even more difficult. As I began writing my own book I recognized this generic truth. If one lives long enough one has not only a story to share, but a philosophy. Mine came about at midlife during a period of monumental soul questioning and searing self-doubt over whether to make my book the final chapter in my teaching career.

The Book for Math Empowerment: Rethinking the Subject of Mathematics came about incrementally over a period of nine months beginning in 1995. Taking the advice of teacher-writer Brenda Ueland (now deceased), I just put it on the page without regard to chapter sequence or outline, and later wove the fragments together into eight cohesive chapters. As I think back, it was a risky way to write a first book, but a creative methodology I will use again and again. Inspired by creativity guru Julia Cameron, I had not only the desire to write, but to paint. *The Book for Math Empowerment* evolved amidst the creation of purple and fuchsia abstracts, which now hang interspersed among my husband's oil paintings in our home. (Donald is the real artist.) However, driven to paint and driven to write, time created itself as I continued my life, scurrying between Stafford and Annandale on Route I95, trying to bring math to life for students at Northern Virginia Community College. What I said I wrote. What I wrote I spoke. The classroom experience, the book, and I became one. Wed within 112 pages are my philosophies of excellence, paradigms for self-transformation, affirmations, and tips on effective teaching and parenting. Getting all of this to flow together in what others have described as easy, thoughtful reading was nothing short of miraculous.

That ..."It was like a gift from God," spoken easily by a woman I had never seen before was my dearest compliment. But, what I hear most often is a simple "I liked it." My neighbor said it gave her the courage to return to college. One of my friends and colleagues sees it as a major tool for healing students' woes. With all of the positive feedback the book is receiving, one thing concerns me as a writer-idealist-pragmatist. If it really has the potential to help people and change lives, why were so many publishers willing to overlook that fact? Like so many new writers I had been met with over two dozen rejections before choosing to self-publish. Had I continued to submit my manuscript, I am certain that there would have been two dozen more.

HOWEVER, THE DECISION TO SELF-PUBLISH CHALLENGED ME LIKE NO OTHER LEARNING EXPERIENCE. There were three months of agonizing attention to the details of editing, rewriting, and contracting with a printer, photographer, and graphic artist. Next, I was required to master the paper trail dictated by the Office of Copyright, Library of Congress, and ISBN Corporation. Compared to getting a master's degree, getting the book published was harder than hard. However, I did it and have a new respect for the acknowledgements page in every book.

Now upon entering a library or bookstore I mentally say to all of the books that greet me, "How ever did all of you get here." I marvel that someone(s) spent thousands of hours (not to mention thousands of dollars) creating a single manuscript and packaging it in the hope that it would engage, entertain, or empower the rest of us. What a gift!

Fragments of a Woman's Life

$\mathscr{I}$am in a recording studio with Patrick, his friend, George, and George's friend, Michelle. While crisscrossing Atlanta's highways we lost Elena, Patrick's dancing partner. The recording studio is hidden in a corner office behind a shopping center. On the floor and surrounding the center sit about thirty people, all of whom are in their mid 20's. Elena shows up between songs number 2 and 3. The wall behind the performer is cloaked with a black acoustical curtain and, besides the white and green ceiling lights are six fat candles burning slowly, setting a warmer atmosphere. Between songs, the vocalist engages in a largely one-sided informal conversation. There is laughter and comfortable companionship to be felt. Each song is introduced with a short background story. He is a wonderful soloist and guitar player, someone Patrick knew from UVA four years earlier. I thought for a moment that he said he was a doctor. If so, he is a very cute one. Patrick, I know, is enthralled, not only because the singer is a friend, but because Patrick, too, is a singer.

This is a part of Patrick's life in Atlanta that I am seeing for the first time, and I am enjoying it.

On the second night of my visit we go to a dance studio. We have chosen not to wait for his friends at the American Legion Hall where everyone is too old and too different for me to have a comfortable evening. I don't want to eat here and I certainly do not want to spend the evening no matter what band is playing. Patrick accommodates me and we go to one of his more habitual haunts. The studio is old and dark inside. There is a pool table, a lowered dance floor and many places to sit. For a brief time I watch. Later on Patrick pulls me onto the floor.

80

Amazingly, I can still swing dance. It is a form I have not invoked for over thirty years. My feet still remember where to go. I dance with another dancer. His style is wider and more languid than Patrick's. I do not enjoy dancing as much with him, but am flattered that he is willing to dance with Patrick's mother. The DJ makes a warm reference to my being there. The hall is practically empty, but we have a good time anyway. I have never seen Patrick quite so sharp. He is wearing his pin-striped black slacks, white shirt and tie, his black hat and black topcoat. After entering, he sheds the coat but keeps the hat. His shoes are those two-toned black and white models one sees in movies of the 30's and 40's. He is as "sharp as a tack" as my mother would say. Patrick burns up the dance floor with another dancer. He is really very good. I hope Patrick gets to do more commercials. I hope he gets to use his talents more. The physics pales in contrast to his ability to sing and dance.

𝒟ear Dawn and Patrick,

I am so very proud of you both, but not only for the reasons you think. I am proud of you because you each have the courage to create the lives you want to live. Doing so requires tremendous strength of character, focus, purpose and commitment. It is much easier to allow someone else to tell you what you should be doing and much more difficult to create your own path.

Dad and I raised you as best we could, given all the crisscrossing agendas in our lives. There are not too many regrets I have, except I wish that I had gotten to know you both better when you were little; that I'd gotten to know the "little Patrick." However, I adore the "big Patrick" a lot! In fact, he is pretty fabulous!

Dawn, diva, you are a magnificent creature, inside and out. I hope in your life you will find someone who cherishes the gemstone within. There exists in you a sacred light that comes forth as gentleness and love that is so very beautiful.

Patrick, please sing and dance every chance you get, and if you get "discovered" on the road to your Ph.D. --- go for it! There is no greater joy than watching you both on stage performing!

Life has much joy to offer those who are looking for it. Embrace life boldly. Step high, and be proud of yourselves. You are both magnificent beings, and I love you very much.

Always,

Mom

Part Seven

Epilogue

Remembering Our Legacies to Embrace a New Millennium

Presented by Sandra Manigault
Metropolitan AME Church
Washington, North Carolina
October 10, 1999

When asked to be your homecoming speaker, I had no choice but to say "yes." Although I have never lived in North Carolina, I have a lot of history here. One could say that my legacies began here in this town. You see, my great-grandmother, Sally Gorham, was one of the founders of this church. My grandmother, Annie Moore Williams had roots here, as did my mother, Jacqueline Young. In 1980, when my parents Silas and Jacqueline Young retired, they made their home here, in Little Washington, and my father still sings in the choir.

When I think about legacies, I have a lot to remember and cherish, and what comes to mind are the values with which I grew up. These are common values, yours and mine, and I'd like to spend some time sharing them with you. Each of them is important if you and I are to embrace the next millenium empowered and focused.

What are our legacies? What have our parents, grandparents, and great-grandparents given to us that has sustained us so far, and will sustain us as we enter the year 2000?

There are many of them and I would like to start with the first legacy, a **legacy called faith.** We all know the adage, "You can if you think you can." That is a statement of faith.

My mother had the faith that one day I would become a teacher. She believed that with all her heart and never gave up the vision. While all of my peers attended the neighborhood high school, John Adams, she went out of her way to learn all she could about a magnet school, called the High School of Music and Art.

84

It was a high school for musically and artistically gifted students, that was run like an elite private school, even though it was a public high school under the auspices of the New York City Board of Education. My parents groomed me for admission and worked diligently to make it possible for me to succeed there. Attending this school turned out to be the most enriching of all of my educational experiences.

It was very challenging to travel 75-90 minutes a day taking 1 bus and 3 trains to get there each day. But Mom had a vision and the faith to bring it about. There is no doubt that going there changed my life.

My parents had faith. They believed God had a purpose and plan for their lives. Furthermore, they believed that if I got a good education, I could have a better life, and a brighter career path; that I could generate new legacies for the next generation.

When we are children and teenagers, we don't always understand why our parents are pushing us in a certain direction. We do not understand or do not want to understand their motives. But, what needs to be realized is that maybe, just maybe their broader vision is God-driven. That their vision for us is God-sent! That they have faith in us, and that their faith will be a very important part of our ultimate success.

The second legacy was love. I grew up surrounded by love. It embraced everything I did or was not allowed to do. It manifested itself not only in the things I got, but in the guidance I received all of the years that I was in school. That my parents were always there for me, gave me a very strong feeling of security as I was growing up.

The love between my parents was a very real part of my younger life too. I learned a lot from their marriage --- things that I have tried to manifest in my own marriage. I learned how important it is to wait for the right person; someone who will be your helpmate and soul-mate. Someone you respect and trust. Someone with the same value system as yourself.

So, to those of you who aren't married but looking, or who will be looking in the next few years, I say don't rush and <u>don't settle for less than God's best</u>. Let God be in the plans.

In my own experiences, love was manifested on a deeper level as well. My parents set the example of how to be a good parent by showering me consideration, thoughtfulness, and generosity. They modeled for me what good parenting meant: creating a safe haven at home and making sacrifices. It meant visiting the school before something went wrong, and getting to know my teachers so we could talk together about what was going on in class. Good parenting meant helping with homework and securing outside assistance when necessary. It meant not taking "no" for an answer where my well being was concerned. This is what my parents did for me, and what Donald and I have tried to do for our children as well.

The third legacy was kindness. My father is the kindest person I know. When you live with a kind and gentle-spirited person, you are blessed, for they are sensitive to your needs, moods, and respect your space. Growing up in a home in which I was believed in, a home filled with love, kindness, and patience was one of my richest blessings.

The fourth was joy. If you knew my mother, you know that she knew how to enjoy life. She made friends everywhere she went because she truly loved people. She knew how to listen and how to laugh. Mommie knew that with generosity of spirit and joy, life could be lived to the fullest.

The fifth legacy was persistence. Had my parents not taught me about persistence, I would never have succeeded at anything. There is a saying: "When the going gets tough, the tough get going." Another popular saying is "Winners don't quit and quitters don't win." I believe them both!

Preparing children for the next millennium means teaching them the power of persistence. The world of the next century will be more competitive than ever. Not only will our children need a competitive edge, they will need the faith to see things through.

They will need to know that getting what you want will mean working harder, longer, smarter, and more consistently. They will need to know that you cannot give up your goals just because getting something is difficult.

The sixth legacy was to strive for excellence. *To you students* I want to say, it is *not enough* for you to merely pass your courses. It is *not enough* for you to be reading on grade level. You have to enjoy reading. You have to have a thirst for knowledge! You *need to excel* at what you do. The world of the next century requires it! My parents instilled in me the desire for excellence: the notion that I had to be better than average. That extra effort we see when someone has won a race or earned the most points in the game, is the same effort that needs to be expended when it comes to school. As my husband describes it, "We need to learn to move beyond the competition!" Striving for excellence is something I did and something we taught our children how to do.

I remember telling our own children, Dawn and Patrick, what it meant to be an adult. I said to them, *"You're an adult when what you think means more than what others think; when you believe in the power of your own opinion." "When you have the courage to be an individual, the courage to back away form the crowd."*

The right to be independent; the presence of mind to stand up for what I believed in; to think for myself --- these are my legacies and my values, and the values we instilled in Dawn and Patrick.

Today's world has too many distractions and too many agendas. Many of these agendas conflict with our values as Christians, as African-Americans, as parents, and as students. We have to learn how to live intelligently. We cannot give into rampant materialism and stupidity just because it is all around us. If we try to buy everything we see, do what everyone else is doing, and keep up with the Joneses, we will go broke, and become stressed and unhappy. The right to be independent is a very important legacy to pass along to our children.

87

Other legacies that have enriched and sustained my life are **the legacies of fairness and honesty.** My parents had an enormous amount of principle and integrity. I can still hear my mother say, "Your word is your bond," and "Never let anyone be any nicer to you than you are to them!" Honesty is very important to Daddy, who says, "If you'll lie, you'll steal!" I clearly remember watching my parents do the right thing in all situations, no matter how costly or inconvenient it was at the time. I was taught that integrity is a vital part of successful living. However, what we must remember is that these values --- integrity, honesty, and fairness are peculiar things. You cannot just talk about them. You have to <u>live</u> them.

My parents believed in doing "first things first." What are we talking about here? Priorities! Taking care of business! Teaching a child the value of doing "first things first" sets the stage for better discipline and organization and puts life in proper sequential order. "First things first" means homework gets done, tests get studied for, rooms get cleaned up, grades stay in the A – B range. It means high GPA's and, ultimately, scholarships to college. It is a powerful legacy to pass on.

As a young woman, **I was always taught to take myself and life seriously.** That unnecessary mistakes could be avoided by taking sound advice from someone who knew more than I knew. That what we are doing here in our lives is no dress rehearsal. That life is serious business. My parents did not take any foolishness either when it came to the young men I dated. Every one of them had to pass the litmus test. Donald remembers. He had to pass it too!

My parents taught me the spirit of cooperation. As parents they worked together at everything. They kept no secrets from each other and shared jointly in the responsibility of running our home. There was none of this "my job, your job," or "my money, your money" stuff. They were a team. That kind of cooperation is what makes a marriage last. It was a powerful legacy to pass on.

I am forever grateful to my parents for giving me all the things I have mentioned plus **an appreciation for the arts:** visual art, classical music, live theatre. That legacy, a love of the arts, has already passed down to the next generation in our family. Our daughter will be a professional ballet/modern dancer after she receives her BFA from college in the spring. She will be the first one in the family to have carved out a creative career in the performing arts.

The legacies continue. **The value of family, of education, of cultivating the inner self, the inner person** are very vivid in my mind. I can still hear the admonitions, "Get your education. Get your education." "It's not what's on the outside of your head that matters. It's what's on the inside!" It was this kind of thinking that helped me to get my master's degree at the age of 22, and is helping our son get his Ph.D. next year. This is the kind of thinking that will get our people through the next millennium.

I cannot close without mentioning the **legacy of prayer.** I am sure that each of you remembers seeing your parents on their knees. They knew that God was the source of their strength and their success. God has brought all of our families a mighty long way and the greatest miracle of all, is that we, as African Americans, survived!

As we move into the next millennium, let us remember to take with us the power and habit of prayer. Prayer makes us strong, whole, focused and free. Free to re-define our lives <u>and</u> to do God's will; for our will, <u>will be</u> God's Will, and our vision, God's mission for our lives.

I have shared some of my legacies with you, which I believe are your legacies too. As a final word I would like to give each letter of the word "legacy" some special meaning for our young people.

L stands for listen. Learn to listen. Listen to your parents and listen to the still, small voice, the voice of God within you.

E: **E stands for evolve**. Today, work to be a little better than you were yesterday, and tomorrow, try to be better than you a today.

G: **G stands for give.** Give your best. Never undermine your God given abilities by doing less than what you are able.

A: **A stands for attitude**. Accentuate the positive. Be an upbeat person. Learn to live with a positive attitude and appreciate the good in your life.

C: **C stands for Christ**. Live a Christian life. Don't go off to college and forget who you are.

Y: **Y stands for yield.** Yield. Be willing to find out why God put you where you are and, when you do, yield yourself to that Higher Purpose for living.

Good luck and Godspeed.

More about the author ---

Sandra Manigault, B.S., M.A., attended Long Island University and Pennsylvania State University. She has taught mathematics at the high school and community college levels in both New York City and Fairfax, Virginia. Over the years, she has assisted her husband run their educational business, *The Manigault Institute*, taught preparation courses for the SAT, written curricula, and presented numerous workshops for teachers, parents, and students. She is a conference facilitator and offers workshops addressing the development of scholars and personal empowerment. Among her favorite workshops are

1. "Is There A Book in You?"
2. "Connecting With a Hostile Audience: Teaching the Math Scared"
3. "Personal Transformation: Creating the Life You Want to Live"

She is currently teaching mathematics at Northern Virginia Community College and still writing.

About the artist ---

Donald Manigault has been painting in oils an
acrylics for more than three decades. His brilliant abstract
utilize several themes, many of them metaphysica
Complex designs and bold color dominate his style, whic
can be described best as esoteric. Regarding his ar
according to one of his friends, "Donald knows a lot of stu
he doesn't tell." He has exhibited his work in various ar
shows, largely in the Virginia area.

The multi-talented artist is additionally an educato
who is committed to the development of human potentia
through many vehicles. He has spent many years teachin
mathematics, working as a school administrator an
developing courses and workshops for his business, Th
Manigault Institute. He is an outstanding motivator an
works with students and parents to develop scholars. I
addition to the above, he finds time to create wealth fo
others using the internet.

His latest artistic ventures are a new book, *Art i
Black and White: a Collage of Thoughts and Images* an
Foray into Creativity, a workshop merging meditation, ar
and writing.

ORDER FORM

Did you enjoy reading this book? Would you like to share it with others?

To order copies of Fragments of a Woman's Life ---
A Memoir

Make your check or money order payable to
Godosan Publications, Inc. and mail to

Godosan Publications, Inc.
P.O. Box 3267
Stafford, Virginia 22555
(540)720-0861, phone and fax
e-mail: godosan@bigplanet.com

Note: *the cost is $12.95 per book,* plus $3 shipping and
handling for the first book and $1 for each additional book.

I am ordering _____ *copies of* **Fragments of a Woman's Life**

Name _____

Address _____

City, State, Zip Code _____

_____

Phone _____

e-mail _____

Book total _____ _Shipping total _____

4.5% Sales tax (Virginia Residents only) _____

Total enclosed _____

To learn more about how you can invite Sandra to give a workshop
for your organization or speak at your conference, please call
(540)720-0861 or e-mail her at godosan@bigplanet.com

More About <u>The Book for Math Empowerment: Rethinking</u>
<u>the Subject of Mathematics</u>
By Sandra Manigault

Many people struggle needlessly because they are intimidated by the subject of mathematics. I have see countless adult students put their lives on hold while they d everything possible to avoid taking a single math course. have seen children suffer poor self-concepts, believin something was wrong with them, because they could no understand how to do math.

<u>The Book for Math Empowerment</u> was written to hel all of these people. Using affirmations, an examination o our belief systems, successful mentoring/teachin techniques, and much more, it addresses how we can succee in mathematics. Chapter by chapter, the reader is give much to ponder and consider, until finally, the mystiqu that has surrounded the subject falls away.

It is not a textbook and I make no attempt to teac you how to do fractions or solve equations. What I *do* is t shed some light on a much misunderstood subject b examining the psychology of learning it: by givin strategies and exercises to overcome the resistance that ha been built up over the years.

For a more detailed description of the book, pleas write for an abstract and book review, or consult our we site.

You will want to order the book that readers hav described as powerful, insightful, innovative, an inspirational.

The author

ORDER FORM

Would you like to understand the psychology of learning mathematics? Would you like to share the inspiration found in *The Book for Math Empowerment?*

To order, send your check or money order for $ 12.95 per book plus $ 3 for shipping & handling ($1, s & h each additional book)

To: **Godosan Publications, Inc.**
       P.O. Box 3267
       Stafford, Virginia 22555
       (540)720-0861

I am ordering ____ copies of *The Book for Math Empowerment*

Name _____
Address _____
City, State, Zip code _____
Phone _____
e-mail _____
Book total _____ Shipping total _____
4.5% sales tax on books (VA residents only) _____
Total enclosed _____

To learn how you can invite Sandra to give a workshop for your school or organization, you may e-mail her at
                                        sandra.manigault@gmail.com
   Web address for **The** :
              www.myplanet.net/godosan

ORDER FORM

Did you enjoy reading this book? Would you like to share it with others?

*To order copies of Fragments of a Woman's Life ---
A Memoir*

Make your check or money order payable to
Godosan Publications, Inc. and mail to

**Godosan Publications, Inc.
P.O. Box 3267
Stafford, Virginia 22555
(540)720-0861, phone and fax**
e-mail:

ALL BOOKS AVAILABLE at
sandralynnlegacies.com
FREE SHIPPING *k,* plus $3 shipping and
handling for the first book and $1 for each additional book.

I am ordering _____ *copies of* **Fragments of a Woman's Life**

Name _____
Address _____
City, State, Zip Code _____
_____
Phone _____
e-mail _____
Book total _____   Shipping total _____
4.5% Sales tax (Virginia Residents only) _____
Total enclosed _____

*To learn more about how you can invite Sandra to give a workshop
for your organization or speak at your conference, please call
(540)720-0861 or e-mail her*

sandra.manigault@gmail.com